LEFT & RIGHT:

THE PROSPECTS FOR LIBERTY

LEFT &
RIGHT:

THE PROSPECTS
FOR LIBERTY

MURRAY N. ROTHBARD

MISES INSTITUTE

Ludwig von Mises Institute
518 West Magnolia Avenue
Auburn, Alabama 36832
mises.org

Large Print Edition published 2012 by Skyler J. Collins. Visit: www.skylerjcollins.com

Cover image by StockFreeImages.com.

ISBN-13: 978-1479349951
ISBN-10: 147934995X

Left and Right:
The Prospects for Liberty

THE CONSERVATIVE HAS LONG BEEN MARKED, whether he knows it or not, by long-run pessimism: by the belief that the long-run trend, and therefore Time itself, is against him, and hence the inevitable trend runs toward left-wing statism at home and Communism abroad. It is this long-run despair that accounts for the Conservative's rather bizarre short-run optimism; for since the long run is given up as hopeless, the Conservative feels that his only hope of success rests in the current moment. In foreign affairs, this point of view leads the Conservative to call for desperate showdowns with Communism, for he feels that the longer he waits the worse things will ineluctably become; at home, it leads him to total concentration on the very next election, where he is always hoping for victory and never

Originally appeared in *Left and Right* (Spring 1965): 4–22.

achieving it. The quintessence of the Practical Man, and beset by long-run despair, the Conservative refuses to think or plan beyond the election of the day.

Pessimism, however, both short-run and long-run, is precisely what the prognosis of Conservatism deserves; for Conservatism is a dying remnant of the *ancien régime* of the preindustrial era, and, as such, it has no future. In its contemporary American form, the recent Conservative Revival embodied the death throes of an ineluctably moribund, Fundamentalist, rural, small-town, white Anglo-Saxon America. What, however, of the prospects for liberty? For too many libertarians mistakenly link the prognosis for liberty with that of the seemingly stronger and supposedly allied Conservative movement; this linkage makes the characteristic long-run pessimism of the modern libertarian easy to understand. But this paper contends that, while the short-run prospects for liberty at home and abroad may seem dim, the proper attitude for the libertarian to take is that of unquenchable long-run optimism.

The case for this assertion rests on a certain view of history: which holds, first, that before the eighteenth century in Western Europe there existed (and still continues to exist outside the

West) an identifiable Old Order. Whether the Old Order took the form of feudalism or Oriental despotism, it was marked by tyranny, exploitation, stagnation, fixed caste, and hopelessness and starvation for the bulk of the population. In sum, life was "nasty, brutish, and short"; here was Maine's "society of status" and Spencer's "military society." The ruling classes, or castes, governed by conquest and by getting the masses to believe in the alleged divine imprimatur to their rule.

The Old Order was, and still remains, the great and mighty enemy of liberty; and it was particularly mighty in the past because there was then no inevitability about its overthrow. When we consider that basically the Old Order had existed since the dawn of history, in all civilizations, we can appreciate even more the glory and the magnitude of the triumph of the liberal revolution of and around the 18th century.

Part of the dimensions of this struggle has been obscured by a great myth of the history of Western Europe implanted by antiliberal German historians of the late nineteenth century. The myth held that the growth of absolute monarchies and of mercantilism in the early modern era was necessary for the development of capitalism, since these served to liberate the merchants and the people from local feudal restrictions. In actuality, this was not at all the case; the King and his nation-State served rather as a superfeudal overlord re-imposing and reinforcing feudalism just as it was being dissolved by the peaceful growth of the market economy. The King superimposed his own restrictions and monopoly privileges onto those of the feudal regime. The absolute monarchs were the Old Order writ large and made even more despotic than before. Capitalism, indeed, flourished earliest and most actively precisely in those areas where the central State was weak or non-existent: the Italian cities, the Hanseatic League, the confederation of seventeenth century Holland. Finally, the old order was overthrown or severely shaken in its grip in two ways. One was by industry and the market expanding through the interstices of the feudal order (e.g., industry in England developing in the countryside beyond the grip of feudal, State, and guild restrictions.) More important was a series of cataclysmic revolutions that blasted loose the Old Order and the old ruling classes: the English Revolutions of the seventeenth century, the American Revolution, and the French Revolution, all of which were necessary to the ushering in of the Industrial Revolution and of at least partial victories for individual liberty, laissez-faire separation of church-and-state, and international peace. The society of status gave way, at least partially, to the "society of contract"; the military society gave way partially to the "industrial society." The mass of the population now achieved a mobility of labor and place, and accelerating expansion of their living standards, for which they had scarcely dared to hope. Liberalism had indeed brought to the Western world not only liberty, the prospect of peace, and the rising living standards of an industrial society, but above all perhaps, it brought hope, a hope in ever-greater progress that lifted the mass of mankind out of its age-old sink of stagnation and despair.

Soon there developed in Western Europe two great political ideologies, centered around this new revolutionary phenomenon: the one was Liberalism, the party of hope, of radicalism, of liberty, of the Industrial Revolution, of progress, of humanity; the other was Conservatism, the party of reaction, the party that longed to restore the hierarchy, statism, theocracy, serfdom, and class exploitation of the old order. Since liberalism admittedly had reason on its side, the Conservatives darkened the ideological atmosphere with obscurantist calls for romanticism, tradition, theocracy, and irrationalism. Political ideologies were polarized, with Liberalism on the extreme "Left," and Conservatism on the extreme "Right," of the ideological spectrum. That genuine Liberalism was essentially radical and revolutionary was brilliantly perceived, in the twilight of its impact, by the great Lord Acton (one of the few figures in the history of thought who, charmingly, grew more radical as he grew older). Acton wrote that "Liberalism wishes for what ought to be, irrespective of what is." In working out this view, incidentally, it was Acton, not Trotsky, who first arrived at the concept of the "permanent revolution." As Gertrude Himmelfarb wrote, in her excellent study of Acton:

> his philosophy develop[ed] to the point where the future was seen as the avowed enemy of the past, and where the past was allowed no authority except as it happened to conform to morality. To take seriously this Liberal theory of history, to give precedence to "what ought to be" over "what is," was, he admitted, virtually to install a "revolution in permanence."

The "revolution in permanence," as Acton hinted in the inaugural lecture and admitted frankly in his notes, was the culmination of his philosophy of history and theory of politics. ... This idea of conscience, that men carry about with them the knowledge of good and evil, is the very root of revolution, for it destroys the sanctity of the past. ... "Liberalism is essentially revolutionary," Acton observed. "Facts must yield to ideas. Peaceably and patiently if possible. Violently if not."[1]

The Liberal, wrote Acton, far surpassed the Whig:

> The Whig governed by compromise. The Liberal begins the reign of ideas. ... One is practical, gradual, ready for compromise. The other works out a principle philosophically. One is a policy aiming at a philosophy. The other is a philosophy seeking a policy.[2]

What happened to Liberalism? Why then did it decline during the nineteenth century? This question has been pondered many times, but perhaps the basic reason was an inner rot within the vitals of Liberalism itself. For, with the partial success of the Liberal Revolution in the West, the Liberals increasingly abandoned their radical fervor, and therefore their liberal goals, to rest content with a mere defense of

---

[1] Gertrude Himmelfarb, *Lord Acton* (Chicago: University of Chicago Press, 1962), pp. 204–05.

[2] Ibid., p. 209.

the uninspiring and defective status quo. Two philosophical roots of this decay may be discerned: First, the abandonment of natural rights and "higher law" theory for utilitarianism. For only forms of natural or higher law theory can provide a radical base outside the existing system from which to challenge the status quo; and only such theory furnishes a sense of necessary immediacy to the libertarian struggle, by focusing on the necessity of bringing existing criminal rulers to the bar of justice. Utilitarians, on the other hand, in abandoning justice for expediency, also abandon immediacy for quiet stagnation and inevitably end up as objective apologists for the existing order.

The second great philosophical influence on the decline of Liberalism was evolutionism, or Social Darwinism, which put the finishing touches to Liberalism as a radical force in society. For the Social Darwinist erroneously saw history and society through the peaceful, rose-colored glasses of infinitely slow, infinitely gradual social evolution. Ignoring the prime fact that no ruling caste in history has ever voluntarily surrendered its power, and that therefore Liberalism had to break through by means of a series of revolutions, the Social Darwinists looked forward peacefully and cheerfully to thousands of years of infinitely gradual evolution to the next supposedly inevitable stage of individualism.

An interesting illustration of a thinker who embodies within himself the decline of Liberalism in the nineteenth century is Herbert Spencer. Spencer began as a magnificently radical liberal, indeed virtually a pure libertarian. But, as the virus of sociology and Social Darwinism took over in his soul, Spencer abandoned libertarianism as a dynamic historical movement, although at first without abandoning it in pure theory. In short, while looking forward to an eventual ideal of pure liberty, Spencer began to see its victory as inevitable, but only after millennia of gradual evolution, and thus, in actual fact, Spencer abandoned Liberalism as a fighting, radical creed; and confined his Liberalism in practice to a weary, rear-guard action against the growing collectivism of the late nineteenth-century. Interestingly enough, Spencer's tired shift "rightward" in strategy soon became a shift rightward in theory as well; so that Spencer abandoned pure liberty even in theory e.g., in repudiating his famous chapter in *Social Statics*, "The Right to Ignore the State."

In England, the classical liberals began their shift from radicalism to quasi-conservatism in the early nineteenth century; a touchstone of this shift was the general British liberal attitude toward the national liberation struggle in Ireland. This struggle was twofold: against British political imperialism, and against feudal landlordism which had been imposed by that imperialism. By their Tory blindness toward the Irish drive for national independence, and especially for peasant property against feudal oppression, the British liberals (including Spencer) symbolized their effective abandonment of genuine Liberalism, which had been virtually born in a struggle against the feudal land system. Only in the United States, the great home of radical liberalism (where feudalism had never been able to take root outside the South), did natural rights and higher law theory, and consequent radical liberal movements, continue in prominence until the mid-nineteenth century. In their different ways, the Jacksonian and Abolitionist movements were the last powerful radical libertarian movements in American life.[3]

Thus, with Liberalism abandoned from within, there was no longer a party of Hope in the Western world, no longer a "Left" movement to lead a struggle against the State and against the unbreached remainder of the Old

---

[3] Cf. Carl Becker, *The Declaration of Independence* (New York: Vintage Books, 1958), chap. VI.

Order. Into this gap, into this void created by the drying up of radical liberalism, there stepped a new movement: Socialism. Libertarians of the present day are accustomed to think of social-ism as the polar opposite of the libertarian creed. But this is a grave mistake, responsible for a severe ideological disorientation of liber-tarians in the present world. As we have seen, Conservatism was the polar opposite of liberty; and socialism, while to the "left" of conserva-tism, was essentially a confused, middle-of-the road movement. It was, and still is, middle-of-the road because it tries to achieve Liberal ends by the use of Conservative means.

In short, Russell Kirk, who claims that Socialism was the heir of classical liberalism, and Ronald Hamowy, who sees Socialism as the heir of Conservatism, are both right; for the question is on what aspect of this confused centrist movement we happen to be focusing. Socialism, like Liberalism and against Con-servatism, accepted the industrial system and the liberal goals of freedom, reason, mobility, progress, higher living standards the masses, and an end to theocracy and war; but it tried to achieve these ends by the use of incompatible, Conservative means: statism, central planning, communitarianism, etc. Or rather, to be more precise, there were from the beginning two different strands within Socialism: one was the Right-wing, authoritarian strand, from Saint-Simon down, which glorified statism, hierarchy, and collectivism and which was thus a projection of Conservatism trying to accept and dominate the new industrial civilization. The other was the Left-wing, relatively libertarian strand, exemplified in their different ways by Marx and Bakunin, revolutionary and far more interested in achieving the libertarian goals of liberalism and socialism: but especially the smashing of the State apparatus to achieve the "withering away of the State" and the "end of the exploitation of man by man." Interestingly enough, the very Marxian phrase, the "replacement of the government of men by the administration of things," can be traced, by a circuitous route, from the great French radical laissez-faire liberals of the early nineteenth century, Charles Comte (no relation to Auguste Comte) and Charles Dunoyer. And so, too, may the concept of the "class struggle"; except that for Dunoyer and Comte the inherently antithetical classes were not businessmen vs. workers, but the producers in society (including free businessmen, workers, peasants, etc.) versus the exploiting classes constituting, and privileged by, the State apparatus.[4] Saint-Simon, at one time in his confused and chaotic life, was close to Comte and Dunoyer and picked up his class analysis from them, in the process characteristically getting the whole thing balled up and converting businessmen on the market, as well as feudal landlords and others of the State privileged, into "exploiters." Marx and Bakunin picked this up from the Saint-Simonians, and the result gravely misled the whole Left Socialist movement; for, then, in addition to smashing the repressive State, it became supposedly necessary to smash private capitalist ownership of the means of production. Rejecting private property, especially of capital, the Left Socialists were then trapped in a crucial inner contradiction: if the State is to disappear after the Revolution (immediately for Bakunin, gradually "withering" for Marx), then

---

[4] The information about Comte and Dunoyer, as well indeed as the entire analysis of the ideological spectrum, I owe to Mr. Leonard P. Liggio. For an emphasis on the positive and dynamic aspect of the Utopian drive, much traduced in our time, see Alan Milchman, "The Social and Political Philosophy of Jean-Jacques Rousseau: Utopia and Ideology," *The November Review* (November, 1964): 3–10. Also cf., Jurgen Ruhle, "The Philosopher of Hope: Ernst Bloch," in Leopold Labedz, ed., *Revisionism* (New York: Praeger, 1962), pp. 166–78.

how is the "collective" to run its property without becoming an enormous State itself in fact even if not in name? This was a contradiction which neither the Marxists nor the Bakuninists were ever able to resolve.

Having replaced radical liberalism as the party of the "Left," Socialism, by the turn of the twentieth century, fell prey to this inner contradiction. Most Socialists (Fabians, Lassalleans, even Marxists) turned sharply rightward, completely abandoned the old libertarian goals and ideals of revolution and the withering away of the State, and became cozy Conservatives permanently reconciled to the State, the status quo, and the whole apparatus of neo-mercantilism, State monopoly capitalism, imperialism and war that was rapidly being established and riveted on European society at the turn of the twentieth century. For Conservatism, too, had re-formed and regrouped to try to cope with a modern industrial system, and had become a refurbished mercantilism, a regime of statism marked by State monopoly privilege, in direct and indirect forms, to favored capitalists and to quasi-feudal landlords. The affinity between Right Socialism and the new Conservatism became very close, the former advocating similar policies but with a demagogic populist veneer: thus, the other side of the coin of imperialism was "social imperialism," which

Joseph Schumpeter trenchantly defined as "an imperialism in which the entrepreneurs and other elements woo the workers by means of social welfare concessions which appear to depend on the success of export monopolism."[5]

Historians have long recognized the affinity, and the welding together, of Right-wing socialism with Conservatism in Italy and Germany, where the fusion was embodied first in Bismarckism and then in Fascism and National Socialism: the latter fulfilling the Conservative program of nationalism, imperialism, militarism, theocracy, and a right-wing collectivism that retained and even cemented the rule of the old privileged classes. But only recently have historians begun to realize that a similar pattern occurred in England and the United States. Thus, Bernard Semmel, in his brilliant history of the social-imperialist movement in England at the turn of the twentieth century, shows how the

---

[5] Joseph A. Schumpeter, *Imperialism and Social Classes* (New York: Meridian Books, 1955), p. 175. Schumpeter, incidentally, realized that, far from being an inherent stage of capitalism, modern imperialism was a throwback to the pre-capitalist imperialism of earlier ages, but with a minority of privileged capitalists now joined to the feudal and military castes in promoting imperialist aggression.

Fabian Society welcomed the rise of the Imperialists in England.[6] When, in the mid-1890s, the Liberal Party in England split into the Radicals on the left and the Liberal-Imperialists on the right, Beatrice Webb, co-leader of the Fabians, denounced the Radicals as "laisser faire and anti-imperialist" while hailing the latter as "collectivists and imperialists." An official Fabian manifesto, *Fabianism and the Empire* (1900), drawn up by George Bernard Shaw (who was later, with perfect consistency, to praise the domestic policies of Stalin and Mussolini and Sir Oswald Mosley), lauded Imperialism and attacked the Radicals, who "still cling to the fixed frontier ideals of individualist republicanism (and) non-interference." In contrast, "a Great Power ... must govern (a world empire) in the interests of civilization as a whole." After this, the Fabians collaborated closely with Tories and Liberal-Imperialists. Indeed, in late 1902, Sidney and Beatrice Webb established a small, secret group of brain-trusters called The Coefficients; as one of the leading members of this club, the Tory imperialist, Leopold S. Amery, revealingly wrote: "Sidney and Beatrice Webb

---

[6] Bernard Semmel, *Imperialism and Social Reform: English Social-Imperial Thought, 1895–1914* (Cambridge: Harvard University press, 1960).

were much more concerned with getting their ideas of the welfare state put into practice by anyone who might be prepared to help, even on the most modest scale, than with the early triumph of an avowedly Socialist Party... . There was, after all, nothing so very unnatural, as (Joseph) Chamberlain's own career had shown, in a combination of Imperialism in external affairs with municipal socialism or semi-socialism at home."[7] Other members of the Coefficients, who, as Amery wrote, were to function as a "Brains Trust or General Staff" for the movement, were: the Liberal-Imperialist Richard B. Haldane; the geo-politician Halford J. Mackinder; the Imperialist and Germanophobe Leopold Maxse, publisher of the *National Review*; the Tory socialist and imperialist Viscount Milner; the naval imperialist Carlyon Bellairs; the famous journalist J.L. Garvin; Bernard Shaw; Sir Clinton Dawkins, partner of the Morgan bank; and Sir Edward Grey, who, at a meeting of the club first adumbrated the policy of Entente with France and Russia that was to eventuate in the First World War.[8]

---

[7] Leopold S. Amery, *My Political Life* (London, 1953), quoted in Semmel, pp. 74–75.

[8] The point, of course, is not that these men were products of some "Fabian conspiracy"; but, on the contrary, that

The famous betrayal, during World War I, of the old ideals of revolutionary pacifism by the European Socialists, and even by the Marxists, should have come as no surprise; that each Socialist Party supported its "own" national government in the war (with the honorable exception of Eugene Victor Debs' Socialist Party in the United States) was the final embodiment of the collapse of the classic Socialist Left. From then on, socialists and quasi-socialists joined Conservatives in a basic amalgam, accepting the State and the Mixed Economy (=neo-Mercantilism=the Welfare State-Interventionism=State Monopoly Capitalism, merely synonyms for the same essential reality). It was in reaction to this collapse that Lenin broke out of the Second International, to re-establish classic revolutionary Marxism in a revival of Left Socialism.

In fact, Lenin, almost without knowing it, accomplished more than this. It is common knowledge that "purifying" movements, eager to return to a classic purity shorn of recent corruptions, generally purify further than what had held true among the original classic sources.

Fabianism, by the turn of the century, was Socialism so conservatized as to be closely aligned with the other dominant neo-Conservative trends in British political life.

There were, indeed, marked "conservative" strains in the writings of Marx and Engels themselves which often justified the State, Western imperialism and aggressive nationalism, and it was these motifs, in the ambivalent views of the Masters on this subject, that provided the fodder for the later shift of the majority Marxists into the "social imperialist" camp.[9] Lenin's camp turned more "left" than had Marx and Engels themselves. Lenin had a decidedly more revolutionary stance toward the State, and consistently defended and supported movements of national liberation against imperialism. The Leninist shift was more "leftist" in other important senses as well. For while Marx had centered his attack on market capitalism per se, the major focus of Lenin's concerns was on what he conceives to be the highest stages of capitalism: imperialism and monopoly. Hence Lenin's focus, centering as it did in practice on State monopoly and imperialism rather than on laissez-faire capitalism, was in that way far more congenial to the libertarian than that of Karl Marx. In recent years, the splits in the Leninist world have brought to the fore a still more left-wing tendency: that of the Chinese.

---

[9] Thus, see Horace B. Davis. "Nations, Colonies, and Social Classes: The Position of Marx and Engels," *Science and Society* (Winter 1965): 26–43.

In their almost exclusive stress on revolution in the undeveloped countries, the Chinese have, in addition to scorning Right-wing Marxist compromises with the State, unerringly centered their hostility on feudal and quasi-feudal landholdings, on monopoly concessions which have enmeshed capital with quasi-feudal land, and on Western imperialism. In this virtual abandonment of the classical Marxist emphasis on the working class, the Maoists have concentrated Leninist efforts more closely on the overthrow of the major bulwarks of the Old Order in the modern world.[10]

Fascism and Nazism were the logical culmination in domestic affairs of the modern drift toward right-wing collectivism. It has become customary among libertarians, as indeed among the Establishment of the West, to regard Fascism and Communism as fundamentally identical. But while both systems were indubitably collectivist, they differed greatly in their socio-economic content. For Communism was a genuine revolutionary movement that ruthlessly displaced and overthrew the old

---

[10] The schismatic wing of the Trotskyist movement embodied in the International Committee for the Fourth International is now the only sect within Marxism-Leninism that continues to stress exclusively the industrial working-class.

ruling élites; while Fascism, on the contrary, cemented into power the old ruling classes. Hence, Fascism was a counter-revolutionary movement that froze a set of monopoly privileges upon society; in short, Fascism was the apotheosis of modern State monopoly capitalism.[11] Here was the reason that Fascism

---

[11] See the penetrating article by Alexander J. Groth, "The 'Isms' in Totalitarianism," *American Political Science Review* (December, 1964): 888–901. Groth writes:

> The Communists ... have generally undertaken measures directly and indirectly uprooting existing socio-economic élites: the landed nobility, business, large sections of the middle class and the peasantry, as well as the bureaucratic élites, the military, the civil service, the judiciary and the diplomatic corps. ... Second, in every instance of Communist seizure of power there has been a significant ideological-propagandistic commitment toward a proletarian or workers' state ... (which) has been accompanied by opportunities for upward social mobility for the economically lowest classes, in terms of education and employment, which invariably have considerably exceeded the opportunities available under previous regimes. Finally, in every case the Communists have attempted to change basically the character of the economic systems which fell under their sway, typically from an agrarian to an industrial economy. ... Fascism (both in the German and Italian versions) ... was socio-economically a counter-revolutionary movement. ... It certainly did not dispossess or annihilate existent socio-economic élites. ... Quite the contrary. Fascism did not arrest the trend toward

proved so attractive (which Communism, of course, never did) to big business interests in the West—openly and unabashedly so in the 1920s and early 1930s.[12]

We are now in a position to apply our analysis to the American scene. Here we encounter a contrasting myth about recent American

---

monopolistic private concentrations in business but instead augmented this tendency ...

Undoubtedly, the Fascist economic system was not a free market economy, and hence not "capitalist" if one wishes to restrict the use of this term to a laissez-faire system. But did it not operate ... to preserve in being, and maintain the material rewards of, the existing socio-economic élites?" (Ibid., pp. 890–91)

[12] For examples of the attractions of Fascist and right-wing collectivist ideas and plans for American big businessmen in this era, see Murray N. Rothbard, *America's Great Depression* (Princeton: Van Nostrand, 1963). Also cf. Gaetano Salvemini and George LaPiana, *What To Do With Italy* (New York: Duell, Sloan, and Pearce, 1943), pp. 65ff.

Of the Fascist economy, Salvemini perceptively wrote: "In actual fact, it is the State, i.e., the taxpayer who has become responsible to private enterprise. In Fascist Italy the State pays for the blunders of private enterprise. ... Profit is private and individual. Loss is public and social." Gaetano Salvemini, *Under the Axe of Fascism* (London: Victor Gollancz, 1936), p. 416.

history which has been propagated by current conservatives and adopted by most American libertarians. The myth goes approximately as follows: America was, more or less, a haven of laissez-faire until the New Deal; then Roosevelt, influenced by Felix Frankfurter, the Intercollegiate Socialist Society, and other "Fabian" and Communist "conspirators," engineered a revolution which set America on the path to Socialism, and, further on, beyond the horizon, to Communism. The present-day libertarian who adopts this or a similar view of the American experience, tends to think of himself as an "extreme right-winger"; slightly to the left of him, then, lies the Conservative, to the left of that the middle-of-the road, and then leftward to Socialism and Communism. Hence, the enormous temptation for some libertarians to red-bait; for, since they see America as drifting inexorably leftward to Socialism and therefore to Communism, the great temptation is for them to overlook the intermediary stages and tar all of their opposition with the hated Red brush.

One would think that the "right-wing libertarian" would quickly be able to see some drastic flaws in this conception. For one thing, the income tax amendment, which he deplores as the beginning of socialism in America, was put through Congress in 1909 by an overwhelming majority of both parties. To look at this event as a sharp leftward move toward socialism would require treating president William Howard Taft, who put through the 16th Amendment, as a Leftist, and surely few would have the temerity to do that. Indeed, the New Deal was not a revolution in any sense; its entire collectivist program was anticipated: proximately by Herbert Hoover during the depression, and, beyond that, by the war-collectivism and central planning that governed America during the First World War. Every element in the New Deal program: central planning, creation of a network of compulsory cartels for industry and agriculture, inflation and credit expansion, artificial raising of wage rates and promotion of unions within the overall monopoly structure, government regulation and ownership, all this had been anticipated and adumbrated during the previous two decades.[13] And this program, with its privileging of various big business interests at the top of the collectivist heap, was in no sense reminiscent of socialism or leftism; there was nothing smacking of the egalitarian or the proletarian here. No, the kinship of this burgeoning collectivism was not at all with Socialism-Communism

---

[13] Thus, see Rothbard, passim.

but with Fascism, or Socialism-of-the-Right, a kinship which many big businessmen of the 'twenties expressed openly in their yearning for abandonment of a quasi-laissez-faire system for a collectivism which they could control. And, surely, William Howard Taft, Woodrow Wilson, and Herbert Clark Hoover make far more recognizable figures as proto-Fascists than they do as crypto-Communists.

The essence of the New Deal was seen, far more clearly than in the conservative mythology, by the Leninist movement in the early 1930s—that is, until the mid-thirties, when the exigencies of Soviet foreign relations caused a sharp shift of the world Communist line to "Popular Front" approval of the New Deal. Thus, in 1934, the British Leninist theoretician R. Palme Dutt published a brief but scathing analysis of the New Deal as "social fascism"—as the reality of Fascism cloaked with a thin veneer of populist demagogy. No conservative opponent has ever delivered a more vigorous or trenchant denunciation of the New Deal. The Roosevelt policy, wrote Dutt, was to "move to a form of dictatorship of a war-type"; the essential policies were to impose a State monopoly capitalism through the NRA, to subsidize business, banking, and agriculture through inflation and the partial expropriation of the mass of the people through lower real wage rates, and to the regulation and exploitation of labor by means of government-fixed wages and compulsory arbitration. When the New Deal, wrote Dutt, is stripped of its "social-reformist 'progressive' camouflage," "the reality of the new Fascist type of system of concentrated state capitalism and industrial servitude remains," including an implicit "advance to war." Dutt effectively concluded with a quote from an editor of the highly respected *Current History Magazine*: "The new America (the editor had written in mid-1933) will not be capitalist in the old sense, nor will it be Socialist. If at the moment the trend is towards Fascism, it will be an American Fascism, embodying the experience, the traditions and the hopes of a great middle-class nation."[14]

Thus, the New Deal was not a qualitative break from the American past; on the contrary, it was merely a quantitative extension of the web of State privilege that had been proposed and acted upon before: in Hoover's Administration, in the war collectivism of World War I, and in the Progressive Era. The most thorough exposition of the origins of State monopoly capitalism, or what he calls "political capitalism," in the

---

[14] R. Palme Dutt, *Fascism and Social Revolution* (New York: International publishers, 1934), pp. 247–51.

U.S. is found in the brilliant work of Dr. Gabriel Kolko. In his *Triumph of Conservatism*, Kolko traces the origins of political capitalism in the "reforms" of the Progressive Era. Orthodox historians have always treated the Progressive period (roughly 1900–1916) as a time when free-market capitalism was becoming increasingly "monopolistic"; in reaction to this reign of monopoly and big business, so the story runs, altruistic intellectuals and far-seeing politicians turned to intervention by the government to reform and regulate these evils. Kolko's great work demonstrates that the reality was almost precisely the opposite of this myth. Despite the wave of mergers and trusts formed around the turn of the century, Kolko reveals, the forces of competition on the free market rapidly vitiated and dissolved these attempts at stabilizing and perpetuating the economic power of big business interests. It was precisely in reaction to their impending defeat at the hands of the competitive storms of the market that business turned, increasingly after the 1900s, to the federal government for aid and protection. In short, the intervention by the federal government was designed, not to curb big business monopoly for the sake of the public weal, but to create monopolies that big business (as well as trade associations smaller business) had not been able to establish amidst the competitive gales of the free market. Both Left and Right have been persistently misled by the notion that intervention by the government is ipso facto leftish and anti-business. Hence the mythology of the New-Fair Deal-as-Red that is endemic on the Right. Both the big businessmen, led by the Morgan interests, and Professor Kolko almost uniquely in the academic world, have realized that monopoly privilege can only be created by the State and not as a result of free market operations.

Thus, Kolko shows that, beginning with Theodore Roosevelt's New Nationalism and culminating in Wilson's New Freedom, in industry after industry, e.g., insurance, banking, meat, exports, and business generally, regulations that present-day Rightists think of as "socialistic" were not only uniformly hailed, but conceived and brought about by big businessmen. This was a conscious effort to fasten upon the economy a cement of subsidy, stabilization, and monopoly privilege. A typical view was that of Andrew Carnegie; deeply concerned about competition in the steel industry, which neither the formation of U.S. Steel nor the famous "Gary Dinners" sponsored by that Morgan company could dampen, Carnegie declared in 1908 that "it always comes back to me that Government control, and that alone, will properly solve the problem." There is nothing alarming about government regulation per se, announced Carnegie, "capital is perfectly safe in the gas company, although it is under court control. So will all capital be, although under Government control."[15]

The Progressive Party, Kolko shows, was basically a Morgan-created party to re-elect Roosevelt and punish President Taft, who had been over-zealous in prosecuting Morgan enterprises; the leftish social workers often unwittingly provided a demagogic veneer for a conservative-statist movement. Wilson's New Freedom, culminating in the creation of

---

[15] See Gabriel Kolko, *The Triumph of Conservatism: A Re-interpretation of American History, 1900–1916* (Glencoe, Ill.: The Free Press, 1963), pp. 173 and passim. For an example of the way in which Kolko has already begun to influence American historiography, see David T. Gilchrist and W. David Lewis, eds., *Economic Change in the Civil War Era* (Greenville, Del.: Eleutherian Mills-Hagley Foundation, 1965), p. 115. Kolko's complementary and confirmatory work on railroads, *Railroads and Regulation, 1877–1916* (Princeton: Princeton University Press, 1965) comes too late to be considered here. A brief treatment of the monopolizing role of the ICC for the railroad industry may be found in Christopher D. Stone, "ICC: Some Reminiscences on the Future of American Transportation," *New Individualist Review* (Spring 1963): 3–15.

the Federal Trade Commission, far from being considered dangerously socialistic by big business, was welcomed enthusiastically as putting their long-cherished program of support, privilege, and regulation of competition into effect (and Wilson's war collectivism was welcomed even more exuberantly.) Edward N. Hurley, Chairman of the Federal Trade Commission and formerly President of the Illinois Manufacturers Association, happily announced, in late 1915, that the Federal Trade Commission was designed "to do for general business" what the ICC had been eagerly doing for the railroads and shippers, what the Federal Reserve was doing for the nation's bankers, and what the Department of Agriculture was accomplishing for the farmers.[16] As would happen more dramatically in European Fascism, each economic interest group was being cartelized and monopolized and fitted into its privileged niche in a hierarchically-ordered socio-economic structure. Particularly influential were the views of Arthur Jerome Eddy, an eminent corporation lawyer who specialized in forming trade associations and who helped to father the Federal Trade Commission. In his magnum opus fiercely denouncing competition in business and

---

[16] Kolko, *Triumph of Conservatism*, p. 274.

calling for governmentally controlled and protected industrial "cooperation," Eddy trumpeted that "Competition is War, and 'War is Hell'."[17]

What of the intellectuals of the Progressive period, damned by the present-day Right as "socialistic"? Socialistic in a sense they were, but what kind of "socialism"? The conservative State Socialism of Bismarck's Germany, the prototype for so much of modern European--and American—political forms, and under which the bulk of American intellectuals of the late nineteenth century received their higher education. As Kolko puts it:

> The conservatism of the contemporary intellectuals ... the idealization of the state by Lester Ward, Richard T. Ely, or Simon N. Patten ... was also the result of the peculiar training of many of the American academics of this period. At the end of the nineteenth century the primary influence in American academic social and economic theory was exerted by the universities. The

---

[17] Arthur Jerome Eddy, *The New Competition: An Examination of the Conditions Underlying the Radical Change That Is Taking Place In the Commercial and Industrial World—The Change from A COMPETITIVE TO A COOPERATIVE BASIS*, 7th ed. (Chicago: A.C. McClurg, 1920).

> Bismarckian idealization of the state, with
> its centralized welfare functions ... was
> suitably revised by the thousands of key
> academics who studied in German univer-
> sities in the 1880s and 1890s.[18]

The ideal of the leading ultra-conservative German professors, moreover, who were also called "socialists of the chair," was consciously to form themselves into the "intellectual body-guard of the House of Hohenzollern"—and that they surely were.

As an exemplar of the Progressive intellectual, Kolko aptly cites Herbert Croly, editor of the Morgan-financed *New Republic*. Systematizing Theodore Roosevelt's New Nationalism, Croly hailed this new Hamiltonianism as a system for collectivist federal control and integration of society into a hierarchical structure.

Looking forward from the Progressive Era, Gabriel Kolko concludes that

> a synthesis of business and politics on the
> federal level was created during the war,
> in various administrative and emergency
> agencies, that continued throughout the
> following decade. Indeed, the war period

---

[18] Kolko, *Triumph of Conservatism*, p. 214.

represents the triumph of business in the most emphatic manner possible ... big business gained total support from the various regulatory agencies and the Executive. It was during the war that effective, working oligopoly and price and market agreements became operational in the dominant sectors of the American economy. The rapid diffusion of power in the economy and relatively easy entry virtually ceased. Despite the cessation of important ... new legislative enactments, the unity of business and the federal government continued throughout the 1920s and thereafter, using the foundations laid in the Progressive Era to stabilize and consolidate conditions within various industries. The principle of utilizing the federal government to stabilize the economy, established in the context of modern industrialism during the Progressive Era, became the basis of political capitalism in its many later ramifications.

In this sense progressivism did not die in the 1920s, but became a part of the basic fabric of American society.[19]

Thus the New Deal. After a bit of leftish wavering in the middle and late 'thirties, the

---

[19] Ibid., pp. 286–87.

Roosevelt Administration re-cemented its alliance with big business in the national defense and war contract economy that began in 1940. This was an economy and a polity that has been ruling America ever since, embodied in the permanent war economy, the full-fledged State monopoly capitalism and neo-mercantilism, the military-industrial complex of the present era. The essential features of American society have not changed since it was thoroughly militarized and politicized in World War II—except that the trends intensify, and even in everyday life men have been increasingly moulded into conforming Organization Men serving the State and its military-industrial complex. William H. Whyte, Jr., in his justly famous book, *The Organization Man*, made clear that this moulding took place amidst the adoption by business of the collectivist views of "enlightened" sociologists and other social engineers. It is also clear that this harmony of views is not simply the result of naiveté by big businessmen—not when such "naiveté" coincides with the requirements of compressing the worker and manager into the mould of willing servitor in the great bureaucracy of the military-industrial machine. And, under the guise of "democracy," education has become mere mass drilling in the techniques of adjustment to the task of becoming a cog in the vast bureaucratic machine.

Meanwhile, the Republicans and Democrats remain as bipartisan in forming and supporting this Establishment as they were in the first two decades of the twentieth century. "Metooism"—bipartisan support of the status quo that underlies the superficial differences between the parties—did not begin in 1940.

How did the corporal's guard of remaining libertarians react to these shifts of the ideological spectrum in America? An instructive answer may be found by looking at the career of one of the great libertarians of twentieth-century America: Albert Jay Nock. In the 1920s, when Nock had formulated his radical libertarian philosophy, he was universally regarded as a member of the extreme left, and he so regarded himself as well. It is always the tendency, in ideological and political life, to center one's attentions on the main enemy of the day, and the main enemy of that day was the conservative statism of the Coolidge-Hoover Administration; it was natural, therefore, for Nock, his friend and fellow libertarian Mencken, and other radicals to join quasi-socialists in battle against the common foe. When the New Deal succeeded Hoover, on the other hand, the milk-and-water socialists and vaguely leftish interventionists hopped on the New Deal bandwagon; on the Left, only the libertarians such as Nock and Mencken, and the Leninists (before the Popular Front period) realized that Roosevelt was only a continuation of Hoover in other rhetoric. It was perfectly natural for the radicals to form a united front against FDR with the older Hoover and Al Smith conservatives who either believed Roosevelt had gone too far or disliked his flamboyant populistic rhetoric. But the problem was that Nock and his fellow radicals, at first properly scornful of their new-found allies, soon began to accept them and even don cheerfully the formerly despised label of "conservative." With the rank-and-file radicals, this shift took place, as have so many transformations of ideology in history, unwittingly and in default of proper ideological leadership; for Nock, and to some extent for Mencken, on the other hand, the problem cut far deeper.

For there had always been one grave flaw in the brilliant and finely-honed libertarian doctrine hammered out in their very different ways by Nock and Mencken; both had long adopted the great error of pessimism. Both saw no hope for the human race ever adopting the system of liberty; despairing of the radical doctrine of liberty ever being applied in practice, each in his own personal way retreated from the responsibility of ideological leadership, Mencken joyously and hedonically, Nock haughtily and secretively. Despite the massive contribution of both men to the cause of liberty, therefore, neither could ever become the conscious leader of a libertarian movement: for neither could ever envision the party of liberty as the party of hope, the party of revolution, or *a fortiori*, the party of secular messianism. The error of pessimism is first step down the slippery slope that leads to Conservatism; and hence it was all too easy for the pessimistic radical Nock, even though still basically a libertarian, to accept the conservative label and even come to croak the old platitude that there is an a priori presumption against any social change.

It is fascinating that Albert Jay Nock thus followed the ideological path of his beloved spiritual ancestor Herbert Spencer; both began as pure radical libertarians, both quickly abandoned radical or revolutionary tactics as embodied in the will to put their theories into practice through mass action, and both eventually glided from Tory tactics to at least a partial Toryism of content.

And so the libertarians, especially in their sense of where they stood in the ideological spectrum, fused with the older conservatives who were forced to adopt libertarian phraseology (but with no real libertarian content) in opposing a Roosevelt Administration that had become too collectivistic for them, either in content or in rhetoric. World War II reinforced and cemented this alliance; for, in contrast to all the previous American wars of the century, the pro-peace and "isolationist" forces were all identified, by their enemies and subsequently by themselves, as men of the "Right." By the end of World War II, it was second nature for libertarians to consider themselves at an "extreme right-wing" pole with the conservatives immediately to the left of them; and hence the great error of the spectrum that persists to this day. In particular, the modern libertarians forgot or never realized that opposition to war and militarism had always been a "left-wing" tradition which had included libertarians; and hence when the historical aberration of the New Deal period corrected itself and the "Right-wing" was once again the great partisan of total war, the libertarians were unprepared to understand what was happening and tailed along in the wake of their supposed conservative "allies." The liberals had completely lost their old ideological markings and guidelines.

Given a proper reorientation of the ideological spectrum, what then would be the prospects for liberty? It is no wonder that the contemporary libertarian, seeing the world going socialist and Communist, and believing himself virtually isolated and cut off from any prospect of united mass action, tends to be steeped in long-run pessimism. But the scene immediately brightens when we realize that that indispensable requisite of modern civilization: the overthrow of the Old Order, was accomplished by mass libertarian action erupting in such great revolutions of the West as the French and American Revolutions, and bringing about the glories of the Industrial Revolution and the advances of liberty, mobility, and rising living standards that we still retain today. Despite the reactionary swings backward to statism, the modern world stands towering above the world of the past. When we consider also that, in one form or another, the Old Order of despotism, feudalism, theocracy and militarism dominated every human civilization until the West of the eighteenth century, optimism over what man has and can achieve must mount still higher.

It might be retorted, however, that this bleak historical record of despotism and stagnation only reinforces one's pessimism, for it shows the persistence and durability of the Old Order and the seeming frailty and evanescence of the New—especially in view of the retrogression of the past century. But such superficial analysis neglects the great change that occurred with the Revolution of the New Order, a change that is clearly irreversible. For the Old Order was able to persist in its slave system for centuries precisely because it awoke no expectations and no hopes in the minds of the submerged masses; their lot was to live and eke out their brutish subsistence in slavery while obeying unquestioningly the commands of their divinely appointed rulers. But the liberal Revolution implanted indelibly in the minds of the masses—not only in the West but in the still feudally-dominated undeveloped world—the burning desire for liberty, for land to the peasantry, for peace between the nations, and, perhaps above all, for the mobility and rising standards of living that can only be brought to them by an industrial civilization. The masses will never again accept the mindless serfdom of the Old Order; and given these demands that have been awakened by liberalism and the Industrial Revolution, long-run victory for liberty is inevitable.

For only liberty, only a free market, can organize and maintain an industrial system, and the more that population expands and explodes, the more necessary is the unfettered working of such an industrial economy. Laissez-faire and the free market become more and more evidently necessary as an industrial system develops; radical deviations cause breakdowns and economic crises. This crisis of statism becomes particularly dramatic and acute in a fully socialist society; and hence the inevitable breakdown of statism has first become strikingly apparent in the countries of the socialist (i.e., Communist) camp. For socialism confronts its inner contradiction most starkly. Desperately, it tries to fulfill its proclaimed goals of industrial growth, higher standards of living for the masses, and eventual withering away of the State, and is increasingly unable to do so with its collectivist means. Hence the inevitable breakdown of socialism. This progressive breakdown of socialist planning was at first partially obscured. For, in every instance the Leninists took power not in a developed capitalist country as Marx had wrongly predicted, but in a country suffering from the oppression of feudalism. Secondly, the Communists did not attempt to impose socialism upon the economy for many years after taking power: in Soviet Russia until Stalin's forced collectivization of the early 1930s reversed the wisdom of Lenin's New Economic Policy, which Lenin's favorite theoretician Bukharin would have extended onward towards a free market. Even the supposedly rabid Communist leaders of China did not impose a socialist economy on that country until the late 1950s. In every case, growing industrialization has imposed a series of economic breakdowns so severe that the Communist countries, against their ideological principles, have had to retreat step by step from central planning and return to various degrees and forms of a free market. The Liberman Plan for the Soviet Union has gained a great deal of publicity; but the inevitable process of de-socialization has proceeded much further in Poland, Hungary, and Czechoslovakia. Most advanced of all is Yugoslavia, which, freed from Stalinist rigidity earlier than its fellows, in only a dozen years has desocialized so fast and so far that its economy is now hardly more socialistic than that of France. The fact that people calling themselves "Communists" are still governing the country is irrelevant to the basic social and economic facts. Central planning in Yugoslavia has virtually disappeared; the private sector not only predominates in agriculture but is even strong in industry, and the public sector itself has been so radically decentralized and placed under free pricing, profit-and-loss tests, and a cooperative worker ownership of each plant that true socialism hardly exists any longer. Only the final step of converting workers' syndical control to individual shares of ownership remains on the path toward outright capitalism. Communist China and the able Marxist theoreticians of *Monthly Review* have clearly discerned the situation and have raised the alarm that Yugoslavia is no longer a socialist country.

One would think that free-market economists would hail the confirmation and increasing relevance of the notable insight of Professor Ludwig von Mises a half-century ago: that socialist States, being necessarily devoid of a genuine price system could not calculate economically and therefore could not plan their economy with any success. Indeed, one follower of Mises in effect predicted this process of de-socialization in a novel some years ago. Yet neither this author nor other free-market economists have given the slightest indication of even recognizing, let alone saluting this process in the Communist countries—perhaps because their almost hysterical view of the alleged threat of Communism prevents them from acknowledging any dissolution in the supposed monolith of menace.[20]

---

[20] One happy exception is William D. Grampp, "New Directions in the Communist Economies," *Business Horizons* (Fall 1963): 29–36. Grampp writes:

Hayek said that centralized planning will lead to serfdom. It follows that a decrease in the economic authority of the State should lead away from serfdom. The Communist countries may show that to

Communist countries, therefore, are increasingly and ineradicably forced to de-socialize, and will therefore eventually reach the free market. The state of the undeveloped countries is also cause for sustained libertarian optimism. For all over the world, the peoples of the undeveloped nations are engaged in revolution to throw off their feudal Old Order. It is true that the United States is doing its mightiest to suppress the very revolutionary process that once brought it and Western Europe out of the shackles of the Old Order; but it is increasingly clear that even overwhelming armed might cannot suppress the desire of the masses to break through into the modern world.

We are left with the United States and the countries of Western Europe. Here, the case for optimism is less clear, for the quasi-collectivist system does not present as stark a crisis of self-contradiction as does socialism. And yet, here too economic crisis looms in the future and gnaws away at the complacency of the Keynesian economic managers: creeping inflation, reflected in the aggravating balance-

---

be true. It would be a withering away of the state the Marxists have not counted on nor has it been anticipated by those who agree with Hayek. (Ibid., p. 35. The novel in question is Henry Hazlitt, *The Great Idea* [New York: Appleton-Century-Crofts, 1951]) of-payments breakdown of the once almighty dollar; creeping secular unemployment brought about by minimum wage scales; and the deeper and long-run accumulation of the uneconomic distortions of the permanent war economy. Moreover, potential crises in the United States are not merely economic; there is a burgeoning and inspiring moral ferment among the youth of America against the fetters of centralized bureaucracy, of mass education in uniformity, and of brutality and oppression exercised by the minions of the State.

Furthermore, the maintenance of a substantial degree of free speech and democratic forms facilitates, at least in the short-run, the possible growth of a libertarian movement. The United States is also fortunate in possessing, even if half-forgotten beneath the statist and tyrannical overlay of the last half-century, a great tradition of libertarian thought and action. The very fact that much of this heritage is still reflected in popular rhetoric, even though stripped of its significance in practice, provides a substantial ideological groundwork for a future party of liberty.

What the Marxists would call the "objective conditions" for the triumph of liberty exist, then, everywhere in the world, and more so than in any past age; for everywhere the masses have opted for higher living standards and the promise of freedom and everywhere the various regimes of statism and collectivism cannot fulfill these goals. What is needed, then, is simply the "subjective conditions" for victory, i.e., a growing body of informed libertarians who will spread the message to the peoples of the world that liberty and the purely free market provide the way out of their problems and crises. Liberty cannot be fully achieved unless libertarians exist in number to guide the peopled to the proper path. But perhaps the greatest stumbling-block to the creation of such a movement is the despair and pessimism typical of the libertarian in today's world. Much of that pessimism is due to his misreading of history and his thinking of himself and his handful of confreres as irredeemably isolated from the masses and therefore from the winds of history. Hence he becomes a lone critic of historical events rather than a person who considers himself as part of a potential movement which can and will make history. The modern libertarian has forgotten that the liberal of the seventeenth and eighteenth centuries faced odds much more overwhelming than faces the liberal of today; for in that era before the Industrial Revolution, the victory of liberalism was far from inevitable. And yet the liberalism of that day was not-content to remain a gloomy little sect; instead, it unified theory and action.

Liberalism grew and developed as an ideology and, leading and guiding the masses, made the Revolution which changed the fate of the world; by its monumental breakthrough, this Revolution of the eighteenth century transformed history from a chronicle of stagnation and despotism to an ongoing movement advancing toward a veritable secular Utopia of liberty and rationality and abundance. The Old Order is dead or moribund; and the reactionary attempts to run a modern society and economy by various throwbacks to the Old Order are doomed to total failure. The liberals of the past have left to modern libertarians a glorious heritage, not only of ideology but of victories against far more devastating odds. The liberals of the past have also left a heritage of the proper strategy and tactics for libertarians to follow: not only by leading rather than remaining aloof from the masses; but also by not falling prey to short-run optimism. For short-run optimism, being unrealistic, leads straightway to disillusion and then to long-run pessimism; just as, on the other side of the coin, long-run pessimism leads to exclusive and self-defeating concentration on immediate and short-run issues. Short-run optimism stems, for one thing, from a naive and simplistic view of strategy: that liberty will win merely by educating more intellectuals, who in turn will educate opinion-moulders, who in turn will convince the masses, after which the State will somehow fold its tent and silently steal away. Matters are not that easy; for libertarians face not only a problem of education but also a problem of power; and it is a law of history that a ruling caste has never voluntarily given up its power.

But the problem of power is, certainly in the United States, far in the future. For the libertarian, the main task of the present epoch is to cast off his needless and debilitating pessimism, to set his sights on long-run victory and to set about the road to its attainment. To do this, he must, perhaps first of all, drastically realign his mistaken view of the ideological spectrum; he must discover who his friends and natural allies are, and above all perhaps, who his enemies are. Armed with this knowledge, let him proceed in the spirit of radical long-run optimism that one of the great figures in the history of libertarian thought, Randolph Bourne, correctly identified as the spirit of youth. Let Bourne's stirring words serve also as the guidepost for the spirit of liberty:

> youth is the incarnation of reason pitted against the rigidity of tradition. Youth puts the remorseless questions to everything that is old and established—Why? What is this thing good for? And when it gets the mumbled, evasive answers of the defenders it

applies its own fresh, clean spirit of reason to institutions, customs, and ideas, and finding them stupid, inane, or poisonous, turns instinctively to overthrow them and build in their place the things with which its visions teem.

Youth is the leaven that keeps all these questioning, testing attitudes fermenting in the world. If it were not for this troublesome activity of youth, with its hatred of sophisms and glosses, its insistence on things as they are, society would die from sheer decay. It is the policy of the older generation as it gets adjusted to the world to hide away the unpleasant things where it can, or preserve a conspiracy of silence and an elaborate pretense that they do not exist. But meanwhile the sores go on festering, just the same. Youth is the drastic antiseptic. ... It drags skeletons from closets and insists that they be explained. No wonder the older generation fears and distrusts the younger. Youth is the avenging Nemesis on its trail ...

Our elders are always optimistic in their views of the present, pessimistic in their views of the future; youth is pessimistic toward the present and gloriously hopeful for the future. And it is this hope which is the lever of progress—one might say, the only lever of progress ...

The secret of life is then that this fine youthful spirit shall never be lost. Out of the turbulence of youth should come this fine precipitate—a sane, strong, aggressive spirit of daring and doing. It must be a flexible, growing spirit, with a hospitality to new ideas, and a keen insight into experience. To keep one's reactions warm and true is to have found the secret of perpetual youth, and perpetual youth is salvation.[21]

---

[21] Randolph Bourne, "Youth," *The Atlantic Monthly* (April 1912); reprinted in Lillian Schlissel, ed., *The World of Randolph Bourne* (New York: E.P. Dutton, 1965), pp. 9–11, 15.